John Henry Menzies, George Hague

On banks and banking in Canada

a study of the bank returns with reference to proposed changes in the bank act

John Henry Menzies, George Hague

On banks and banking in Canada
a study of the bank returns with reference to proposed changes in the bank act

ISBN/EAN: 9783741173646

Manufactured in Europe, USA, Canada, Australia, Japa

Cover: Foto ©knipser5 / pixelio.de

Manufactured and distributed by brebook publishing software
(www.brebook.com)

John Henry Menzies, George Hague

On banks and banking in Canada

ON BANKS AND BANKING IN CANADA:

A STUDY OF THE BANK RETURNS WITH REFERENCE TO PROPOSED CHANGES IN THE BANK ACT.

Treatise:

BY J. H. MENZIES, F.C.A.

WITH PAPERS IN REPLY BY

MR. GEORGE HAGUE, GENERAL MANAGER MERCHANTS BANK OF CANADA,

AND OTHERS.

READ BEFORE THE

Institute of Chartered Accountants of Ontario,

TORONTO, MAY 15th and 22nd, 1890.

PRICE TWENTY-FIVE CENTS.

TORONTO:
WILLIAMSON AND COMPANY.
MONTREAL:
DAWSON BROTHERS.

MAIL JOB PRINT

ON BANKS AND BANKING IN CANADA:

A STUDY OF THE BANK RETURNS WITH REFERENCE TO PROPOSED CHANGES IN THE BANK ACT.

Treatise :

BY J. H. MENZIES, F.C.A.

WITH PAPERS IN REPLY BY

MR. GEORGE HAGUE, GENERAL MANAGER MERCHANTS BANK OF CANADA,

AND OTHERS.

READ BEFORE THE

Institute of Chartered Accountants of Ontario,

TORONTO, MAY 15th and 22nd, 1888.

TORONTO:

WILLIAMSON AND COMPANY.

MONTREAL:

DAWSON BROTHERS.

INSTITUTE

—OF—

Chartered Accountants of Ontario.

Incorporated by Statute of Ontario, 46 Vic., Cap. 64.

OFFICERS.

President :

W. F. FINDLAY, F.C.A., Accountant............................ .*Hamilton.*

Vice-Presidents :

H. W. EDDIS, F.C.A., Accountant.. *Toronto.*
J. T. MOORE, F.C.A., Managing Director Saskatchewan Land and Homestead
    Company .... "

COUNCIL:

WILLIAM MCCABE, F.C.A., F.I.A., F.S.S., Eng., Managing Director North
    American Life Assurance Co...................................... *Toronto.*
E. R. C. CLARKSON, F.C.A., Accountant .... "
S. B. HARMAN, F.C.A., D.C.L., City Treasurer..................... .... "
R. T. COADY, F.C.A., Assistant City Treasurer........................... "
W. H. CROSS, F.C.A., Merchant... "
HON. S. C. WOOD, Manager Freehold Loan and Savings Co. .... "
R. H. TOMLINSON, Manager British Canadian Loan and Investment Co........ "
P. G. ROUTH, Accountant .... "
HUGH SCOTT, Insurance Underwriter .... "
R. JENKINS, Accountant.. "
W. POWIS, F.C.A., Accountant.. .... "
J. J. MASON, F.C.A., Accountant....................................... .*Hamilton.*
A. G. RAMSAY, F.I.A., Eng., Managing Director Canada Life Ins. Co. ..... "
R. L. GUNN, Accountant.. "
G. F. JEWELL, F.C.A., Accountant....................................... *London.*
J. W. JOHNSON, F.C.A., Principal Ontario Business College .... *Belleville.*
HY. LYE, Accountant and Fire Adjuster .... *Cobourg.*
C. A. FLEMING, Principal Northern Business College.................... *Owen Sound.*

AUDITORS :

J. MCARTHUR GRIFFITH,   T. H. MONK.

SECRETARY AND TREASURER:

J. H. MENZIES, F.C.A., Accountant................................... *Toronto.*

On Banks and Banking in Canada.

T HE ACCOMPANYING Analysis* embraces all the more important features of the Returns furnished to Government by the banks. The following observations on the purport of its several columns are offered as a contribution towards the elucidation of a subject of interest not merely to bankers and bank stockholders, but to every commercial man in the country; for no business is quite independent of the banking system.

Financial questions are the practical issues of the day; and it behooves those who are competent to deal with them, or with any branch of them, to give the country any advantage their special knowledge may be worth. In this view the present paper has been written. It does not pretend to exhaust the subject, but merely to furnish some material for discussing it understandingly, in order possibly to the removal of any defects and the after-construction of a perfect banking practice.

C OLUMN ONE of the Analysis shows the extent to which the banks approach the limit of issue ($100 for every $100 of paid-up Capital) allowed by the Bank Act.

BASIS OF CIRCULATION.

THE STATUTORY limitation of the Circulation of the banks to the amount of their unimpaired paid-up Capital is a purely arbitrary one, apparently grounded on no appropriate principle. It is attempted to justify it on the principle, sound in itself, that Credit should be based on Capital. But while credit taken by the banks in the form of Circulation is so limited in amount,

---

* At page 44. In general, the references are to the *January* Returns of the Canadian banks. Analyses of the Returns for February and March are added; and also for comparison in some particulars a similar Analysis of the Returns of a group of English banks—all the London Joint Stock banks furnishing sufficient data for the purpose, whose combined paid-up capital approximates to that of the Canadian banks.

notwithstanding that payment is guaranteed by a first lien on the assets, no limitation is set to the amount of Deposits—that other form of credit taken by the banks without any such guarantee, which is the source from which all legitimate Circulation flows as a stream flows from an upper lake. Thus the reservoir may without check be filled to overflowing, while the capacity of the conduit is to be regulated, and wholly without respect to the volume to be discharged through it. But a bank is authorised to issue Circulation, not by any means because it has an amount invested as bank Capital (for that would warrant the establishment of pure banks of issue, and indeed involves the concession to Government of a right to monopolise the currency), but for the purpose of supplying the country with a suitable currency. The Circulation of a bank is connected, not with the amount of its paid-up Capital, but with the amount of Deposits it holds. A Circulation is created naturally only through the activity of the Deposit account ; and the greater the amount of Deposits, especially Deposits made up of the proceeds of discounts and of business balances, the greater will be the normal Circulation.

In an essay recently published by Mr. W. W. Flannagan, Cashier of the Commercial National Bank, New York, on *The Necessity for a Bank Circulation,* banks and bankers are most aptly styled "dealers in credits." "They handle money as well," says Mr. Flannagan, "but the operations in credits form such a large proportion of the business of banking that it is strictly accurate to say they are dealers in credits ; the money handled being only the reserve or foundation on which the business is conducted. What is classified in a bank statement as ' Deposits' does not necessarily mean money therein deposited. On the contrary, a very small proportion of ' Deposits' represents money deposited. A deposit often is, and usually arises from, a mere exchange of credits ; this exchange may be by checks or drafts on some other banker, or it may be in the nature of a discount, as when the banker takes the 'promise to pay' of his customer which he lists among his assets as ' Bills Discounted,' and gives in exchange therefor his 'promise to pay' which he classes among his liabilities as ' Deposits.' The result is the exchange of one credit payable in the future for another payable on demand. This 'promise to pay' or credit, or deposit, when put into negotiable form so as to pass by delivery without endorsement, is called bank Circulation. It requires no argument to show, for it is apparent in the mere assertion, that Circulation being one form of credit, and bank Deposits another, the demand for the negotiable form, Circulation, will increase *pro rata* with the amount in the form of Deposits. . . . . Bank credits put into the shape of checks and drafts constitute the great bulk of the circulating medium of the country, but the minor operations of trade must necessarily be done with money or bank credits in the form of money (Circulation), and these minor operations keep *pro rata* pace with the larger transactions. So that to the extent that Deposits in banks increase, to the same extent is there a corresponding demand for Circulation."*

While a bank may have a Circulation in due proportion to its Deposits, and only adequate to the currency needs of its customers, the amount may yet far exceed what is allowed by the Bank Act. If the Deposits in the Canadian banks were as large in proportion to the Capital as are the Deposits in the English and Australian banks (to be referred to later), a limitation of the amount of bank Circulation to the amount of paid-up Capital would be altogether inadequate to the currency needs of the country, in default of gold and silver coin : as Deposits grow with the development of the resources of the country, Circulation will grow *pari passu*. And from this it would appear that Capital alone may not be the proper standard to regulate Circulation by ; it might be better, as it would be according to a truer principle, that the legal limit of Circulation should bear a certain proportion also to the amount of Deposits. Under equally good management and in like circumstances, all banks show a pretty uniform proportion of Deposits to Capital, and the Circulation being naturally in *pro rata* proportion to Deposits, it follows ultimately that Circulation also bears a regular proportion to Capital ; and so an objection to the present preferential lien of note-holders, that in case of failure it may absorb an altogether undue proportion of the assets, is obviated.

An indispensable condition should be that adequate Reserves be kept against Circulation as well as Deposits. That would lend support to both, and on such a basis a bank might safely hold any reasonable amount of Deposits with a corresponding Circulation, while restraint would be put on inflation generally, and especially would inflation of Circulation by the discount of bills in order to increase the Deposit account be prevented. With legitimate business methods, the resources of a bank in specie and marketable securities ought to keep pace with the growth of Deposits, and

* The bank bills maintained in Circulation in Canada are mainly in the hands of (1) Farmers and lumbermen, and dealers in agricultural and other natural products; (2) Employers of labor on manufactures, and industrial employers generally ; (3) Shopkeepers ; and (4) The well-to-do classes.
All these except the last two classes get the bank bills directly or indirectly from the banks, generally by way of advances or discounts, sometimes as drafts on actual deposits ; the well-to-do classes get them as drafts on similar deposits, or if in business, also by way of discounts ; city shopkeepers, who hold a very large sum in the aggregate (this in the main is the Circulation created by manufacturers and importers), get them from workpeople and from the well-to-do classes ; country shopkeepers get them from farmers.
It is the aggregate of these sums, kept floating at an average amount by the activities of business, operating through the Deposit account of the banks, that constitutes the bank Circulation.
The Deposit account consists of fixed deposits, the proceeds and balances of proceeds of discounts, and current deposits.
All these constitute the fund from which the banks make advances to the public for use in the domestic trade of the country ; and these advances, with the drafts of the owners of actual deposits, are paid (1) In cheques to pay mercantile indebtedness ; (2) In bank bills and change (Dominion notes and silver), to pay labor in factories, shops, and for industrial disbursements generally ; for purchases of agricultural and other natural products ; and for pocket money.
Bank bills are really change for, and convenient because divisible substitutes for, cheques, just as the smaller Dominion notes and silver is change for bank bills.
Manifestly the volume of Circulation depends altogether on the activity of the Deposit account, through which the fund of fixed deposits is made fluent, with the other deposits, chiefly by the granting of loans as advances and discounts.

therefore of Circulation. And as the credit that attracts Deposits is usually better founded than that which floats currency, the Circulation, while bearing a due proportion to the Deposits, would generally correspond in some measure to the standing of the bank of issue ; and fluctuating with the Deposits as the public gained or lost confidence in the institution, the amount at risk by noteholders would in normal circumstances be automatically adjusted to the degree of credit enjoyed by the bank.

The purpose of Mr. Flannagan's paper is to show that the financial stringency in the States is due, not exclusively or even principally to an excessive Treasury surplus, as is generally supposed, but in a greater measure to a contraction of bank Circulation—the commercial interest of the country being forced under the National bank system to base its medium of exchange, not on the necessities of trade, but on the amount of the decreasing National Debt. And the theory as to the close connexion between Deposits and Circulation appears to be confirmed by a comparison of the figures of the Canadian bank Deposits and Circulation, which since Confederation have shown—save in the years of financial inflation and disturbance, 1871-74—a tolerably uniform proportion the one to the other, as may be seen by the following table, prepared from the Government Returns as given in *The Statistical Abstract and Record, 1886*:

Percentage of Circulation to Deposits.

June 30, 1868....25.3	June 30, 1875......27.8	June 30, 1882....28.3
" 1869....20.8	" 1876.:....27.2	" 1883....30.
" 1870....28.	" 1877......25.6	" 1884....27.8
" 1871....32.9	" 1878......27.	" 1885...28.4
" 1872....38.7	" 1879......25.3	" 1886....25.8
" 1873....42.8	" 1880......23.8	" 1887....26.6
" 1874....33.7	" 1881......27.7	Mch. 31, 1888....28.

During this period, 1868-1888, the Deposits increased from $32,808,103 to $113,938,206, an increase of 248 per cent. ; while the Circulation increased concurrently from $8,307,079 to $31,985,285, an increase of 284 per cent. It appears to be a fair conclusion, therefore, that the normal bank Circulation will in general bear a regular proportion to the amount of the Deposits ; and in the annexed analysis of the February and March Bank Statements I have given the percentage of the one to the other shown by the Returns of the several Canadian banks. This additional column, which I consider the better test of the position of the banks in respect of Circulation, will be found a useful corrective to the one now under notice, whose figures might otherwise, in some cases, convey an erroneous impression of undue inflation of Circulation.

COLUMN TWO shows the proportion of Rest to Capital. This column should be read in connexion with Column One. A high percentage of Circulation as compared with Capital ought in general, for legal requirements, to be accompanied by a high percentage of Rest. Manifestly, where there is little or no Rest, it is impossible, in view of the probable extent of the bank's investments in trade discounts and advances, to affirm that the Capital is unimpaired, unless it is known for certain that all depreciation has been written off ; and therefore in such a case of doubt the legal limit of Circulation ought not to be approached very near, lest the Bank Act be contravened.

RESTS.

THE VALUE of the Rests of Canadian banks depends largely upon the value of the discounted bills, and this it is difficult, perhaps impossible, for one not familiar with the condition and circumstances of each individual discount account to ascertain.

A genuine Rest is usually of slow growth, the result of a cautious and prudent policy steadily pursued ; and its function is to supplement deficient dividends in times of bad business, so as to insure a regular rate of interest to stockholders. To fulfil this purpose properly, however, a bank Rest should be invested, perhaps specifically, in securities other than discounted bills and trade advances : where the profits reserved as Rests are represented by securities of so doubtful a value, they are for the most part but assumed profits, liable to disappear just when a Reserve fund is most needed. In present conditions, indeed, a Canadian bank Rest may usually, to the extent of a certain percentage of the discounted bills, be properly considered as a doubtful surplus reserved against possible bad debts.

The Rest, when realised, if invested as suggested and represented on the other side of the account by an indisputably good asset, might also be made *pro tanto* a guarantee to the stockholders against the possibility in case of disaster of being called upon to pay the amount of their double liability. The double liability is a Reserve of Capital, kept beyond the control of the Management, though not of the bank's creditors, that might be provided against by a special investment ; and if the Rest, in whole or in part, as it accumulated, instead of being divided among the stockholders, as might be done if it were a realised surplus, were invested by statutory authority—vested in trustees, perhaps—for the security and benefit of the stockholders, without depriving the bank of its use in certain investments, of the revenue earned by it, or of any prestige the accumulation of such a fund might afford, such investment, a more tangible security than the double liability resource, being also beyond the control of the Management would be available at need, without further call on the stockholders, to satisfy the double liability claim.

So sure a provision against the hazard of this contingent liability might be expected by attracting investors to have a steadying and most beneficial effect on the price of bank stocks ; and, as I shall presently show, a Rest so invested may be a vastly better security to the creditors of the banks than the double liability fund.

Double Liability.

It may be doubted whether the security afforded to creditors by subjecting bank stockholders to a double liability is at all commensurate with the injury to the public interest caused by what is also a discouragement to investments in bank stocks. The United States Comptroller of the Currency states in his Report for 1887, that the total assessments made in respect of insolvent banks, under the double liability clause, since the institution of the National bank system, have produced only about 47 per cent. gross, the net amount realised to creditors having been under rather than over 40 per cent. It is probable, therefore, that in Canada, where are a much similar body of bank shareholders, the double liability security cannot be counted on as worth on the average more than 40 cents on the dollar, instead of the assumed 100.

Unquestionably, that often calamitous contingent liability strongly repels investors, and is probably a main reason why so much bank stock floats unabsorbed about our stock markets. It certainly is not that more capital stock has been issued than the needs of the country warrant ; but, rather, more has been issued than the investing public will absorb. And until it be absorbed, it cannot be kept off the Stock Exchange, and stock-brokers cannot be prevented from using it for purposes of speculation ; often, possibly, in times of distrust, to the injury of the banks themselves ; at any rate, to the injury of *bona fide* investors, the value of whose property fluctuates with the price of this floating surplus.

COLUMN THREE shows the extent of depreciation in the value of the discounted bills that would absorb the Rest.

This column obviously is one of great importance in estimating the condition of the banks ; but all that can be prudently said about it is said under appropriate headings elsewhere.

COLUMN FOUR shows the extent of depreciation in the value of the discounted bills that would absorb the Capital as well as the Rest.

If the volume of the discounted bills bore a regular proportion to the other assets throughout the series of banks (which, however, it does not, according to Column Six), this column would indicate also the earning power of each bank. To ascertain this, Column Six must be taken into account with this column. Obviously the larger the amount of business a bank can safely do in proportion to the amount of paid-up Capital and Rest, the better the result to the shareholders.

COLUMN FIVE shows the proportion of the working resources of the banks supplied respectively by the stockholders and by the noteholders and the depositors.

EARNING POWER.

A COMPARISON of the figures of the Canadian and the English banks dealt with in the Analyses exhibits the vastly greater earning power enjoyed by the latter. While the paid-up Capital of the Canadian banks is equal to five-sixths the amount of that of the English banks, the Deposits of the Canadian banks amount to little more than one-sixth of the sum held by the English banks. While, too, more than one-half the Deposits in the Canadian banks bear interest, fully two-thirds, in some cases three-fourths, of the Deposits in the English banks are free of interest. For example, in the case of the London and County Bank, having a paid-up Capital of £2,000,000 stg., the Deposits amount to over £29,000,000, at least £20,000,000 of which is non-interest-bearing ; and thus every rate of one per cent. per annum earned by employing this enormous fund yields a dividend of ten per cent. on the paid-up Capital of the Bank. It must be noted, however, that the expenses of such a bank, with its many branches, are proportionately great, amounting in the present case to nearly as much as the dividend paid—20 per cent. per annum ; so that to pay that dividend the Bank must earn a gross profit of near 40 per cent. on its paid-up Capital.

As a partial offset to this advantage of large free Deposits in the English banks, the Canadian banks have a Circulation amounting at present to 32 million dollars, which sum, however, added to the amount of their Deposits, still leaves the balance of advantage in favor of the English banks as nearly four to one. In these favorable circumstances the English banks can well afford to dispense with the profit of a Circulation, especially as they are thereby free from the obligations it might entail.

Owing to the great multitude of the banks in the United States, and the different and differing banking systems there in vogue, we are prevented from drawing any close comparison between the condition of the banks of the two countries in this particular of Deposits : Mr. Flannagan, however, informs us that in August, 1887, the National banks, in number about three thousand (about one-third of the total number of banks in the country), with a paid-up Capital of $572,000,000, held Deposits to the amount of $1,285,000,000. To compare the banks of a comparatively new and poor country like Canada with those of an old and rich one like England, is to compare the affairs of an old-established merchant with the affairs of a new-beginner. And if we turn to our only important sister-colony, Australia, in the endeavor to draw a more equal comparison, we turn to even a richer country than England ; where, so great is the realised wealth, that banks frequently show Deposits to twelve or fifteen-fold the amount of their paid-up Capital. During the past year the bank Deposits there were increased by 38 million dollars, the amount standing to-day at about 470 million, with a population of two and a-half million, against our Deposits of 110 million dollars, with a population nearly double that of Australia.

Such differences illustrate the enormous disadvantages that Canadian banking labors under—a state that would not be improved by an increase of banking capital.

COLUMN SIX shows the proportion of the total resources of the banks employed in discounting bills and in trade advances, thus indicating the relation that mode of investment bears in the practice of the banks to other more readily convertible investments.

It is desirable that the amount of trade discounts and advances should not be in excessive proportion to other investments, nor of course should it exceed the requirements of a healthy state of trade.

COLUMN SEVEN is a measure of the gold-paying ability of the banks, showing the extent of their resources in specie and its equivalents, in funds held abroad, and in securities convertible into gold, available against the possible demands of noteholders and depositors. *

* In producing the figures of this column there have been considered, on the one hand—
Circulation.
Other Deposits payable on demand and after notice.
    Less Notes and cheques of other banks.
        Balances due from other banks in Canada.
            Less Balances due to other banks in Canada.
Dominion Government Deposits payable on demand and after notice.
    Less Loans to Dominion Government.
Provincial Government Deposits payable on demand and after notice.
    Less Loans to Provincial Governments.
Loans from or Deposits made by other banks in Canada, unsecured.
    Less Loans to and Deposits made in other banks in Canada, unsecured.
And on the other hand—
    Specie and Dominion notes.
    Balances due from Agencies or other banks in foreign countries.
        Less Balances due to Agencies or other banks in foreign countries.
    Balances due from Agencies or other banks in the United Kingdom.
        Less Balances due to Agencies or other banks in the United Kingdom.
    Dominion Government Debentures or Stock.
    Provincial, British, Foreign, or Colonial Public Securities other than Canadian.
    Loans, Discounts, or Advances for which stock, bonds, or debentures of Municipal or other Corporations, or Dominion, Provincial, British, or other Public Securities other than Canadian, are held as collateral security.

On March 31, the Canadian banks altogether held, as far as is visible from the Returns, 34.8 per cent. of such resources against their liabilities for Deposits and Circulation.

RESERVES.

THE CANADIAN banking system is peculiarly an edifice of credit, the metallic base on which it rests—the reserve of specie held by the banks in general bearing but a trifling proportion to the liabilities, while other Reserve securities are not in plenty.

While an adequate reserve of gold and equivalent securities is the very corner-stone of safe banking, and the obligation to maintain it must be kept in view constantly, it would yet be a waste for a bank in the circumstances prevailing in Canada to hold in its vaults an excessive amount of specie or bullion, the surplus of which might be invested in interest-bearing securities readily enough available if need should arise.

It is interesting to note how in the practice of commercial peoples the use of credit-money is superseding the use of coin and bullion. Mr. John Thompson, Vice-President of the Chase National Bank, New York, tells us, in a pamphlet lately issued, that (what he appropriately calls) token-money, that is, drafts, checks, letters of credit, etc., now constitutes nineteen-twentieths of business transactions in the States ; and Mr. Gairdner, General Manager of the Union Bank of Scotland, recently pointed out in a paper read before the economic section of the Glasgow Philosophical Society that the Reserves in coin and bullion held by all the banks in the United Kingdom, against liabilities amounting to £613 million sterling, amounted to only £27 million—or about 4½ per cent. of the liabilities. This sum was all that was available to meet demands for inland coin circulation, foreign exchange, and private hoarding. But there was also held by the banks documents representing commodities and securities to the value of £586 million sterling, which would readily enable the banks to increase their stock of gold if need were. So we see that British banking is also in a way no less an edifice of credit. Credit, indeed, and not gold and silver, is the true Reserve of civilisation.

Among the assets of most Canadian banks, it is proper to observe, are considerable amounts of Call Loans and loans at short notice, usually amply secured by convertible securities, part of which, being from lack of discrimination buried in the discounted bills account, are not disclosed by the Returns, but which, nevertheless, ought to be reckoned as readily available against the demands of noteholders and depositors, and added to the percentage of resources shown in Column Seven.

The specie held by all the Canadian banks amounts to six million dollars, and Dominion notes, ten million (out of a total issue of sixteen million, the balance being all the legal tender notes in actual circulation). A net sum of about twelve million dollars is due from agencies in the United States, where that fund is usually employed securely as well as profitably, and a further net tour million is due from agencies in the United Kingdom. The total of such resources so far as visible is $32,356,000; the English banks under notice hold of cash $71,500,000, and Money at Call and short notice $77,000,000—a total of $148,500,000.

Of investments in Government and Public Securities, available in any condition of affairs, the Canadian banks hold to the value of about $6,000,000, the English banks $132,500,000 ; which large holding in this case is partly due to the increasing scarcity of trade bills in England (the plethora of money there telling strongly of late in favor of cash transactions or short credits), and to the prevailing low rates of interest. In these circumstances investments in high class securities are found to prove more profitable than trade advances ; and hence we see that while the discounts and advances of all sorts made by the Canadian banks to the public amount to $167,759,000, these English banks, with their vastly greater resources, show only $418,000,000 of such advances.

The Banks and the Prevailing Commercial System.

APART from Call and Short Loans and bills representing produce and raw materials, the greater portion of the discounted bills held by the Canadian banks may be assumed to be paper representing imports of manufactured goods, and home manufactures. Largely in the purchase of foreign manufactured goods—still more largely in the employment of labor at home and in fostering home industries, has gone the Capital of the banks and the contributions to their resources made by the public by way of Circulation and Deposits; and but a part of this investment is now producible as a liquid asset. Unquestionably, however, property representing it is here in a multiform variety of imports and home manufactures, but not in a shape to be readily converted into gold, to increase the Reserves, except in so far as the goods or representative securities, being still within the control of the banks, may be marketable abroad.

The production of a greater surplus of commodities—of home manufactures and natural products for export, with the open foreign markets our connexion with England may give us, seems to afford the best means of increasing the present bank reserves of gold and equivalent securities. However words may be multiplied theorising about the effect of the Balance of Trade, the elementary truth subsists that a continual excess of Canadian imports over exports certainly tends, Canada being a comparatively poor country *with a large foreign indebtedness*, to drain the country of gold ; and this is evident from the condition of the Canadian bank Reserves as compared with the Reserves of the English banks. And one effect of this condition is, that precisely when ampler accommodation is required from the Canadian banks to pay for these excessive imports—which in default of exports has to be done in gold—and to meet the other demands of a seemingly flourishing state of trade, the resources of the banks being diminished they are compelled to curtail their advances, and the Circulation shrinks correspondingly. The excessive imports of 1870-3, for instance, were followed in the next few years by an absolute decrease in the amount of bank Circulation of 40 per cent.

An apparent illustration of this disabling effect is brought out by comparing the rates of excess of Canadian imports over exports for the period since Confederation, with the Circulation of the banks for the same period. Taking the figures of the Government Returns, as given in *The Statistical Abstract* before quoted, and assuming, as from a consideration of the general course of trade I think we are fairly entitled to do, that such an effect on the business of the banks as I have indicated would not in the nature of things show itself till about the second year after the cause—the over-importation—had come into operation, we find that in every year, save one—1884, when no marked change took place, the effect perhaps not appearing till the next year—an increase or decrease in the excess per head of population of imports over exports—in other words, a worsening or bettering of the balance of foreign trade—has been invariably followed by a more or less corresponding decrease or increase in the Circulation of the banks, as compared with the Capital.*

As compared with the Deposits it will be seen that there are exceptions to this rule at three periods—in 1873, when an increase of Circulation took place, notwithstanding an increase in the rate of excess of imports the previous two years, which was doubtless due to the great inflation of business that prevailed at that time ; in 1880, when the contrary process took place, the Circulation decreasing with a decrease in the rate of excess of imports the previous two years, which may fairly be attributed to the depression in business that reached its height at that date ; and in 1883-5-6, when it is probable the normal Circulation was affected without much respect to the amount of Deposits in the banks by the vast extra expenditures attending the railway works in progress and finishing about that time. It will be

---

It is not the volume of imports that is detrimental, but a continual and great excess of imports over exports, which must be paid for in gold or by contracting foreign debt. To be profitable to both parties there should be no great dissimilarity in the nominal value of imports over exports. The larger the volume of exports, the larger, naturally, will be the volume of imports, and the richer will the country grow by such activity of trade. And the fiscal effect of the volume of exports cannot be considered alone without reference to the volume of imports, nor *vice versa* ; for they are inter-dependent, intimately co-related, and exercise a trong reciprocal influence the one upon the other.

observed, however, that since 1875, the end of a period of financial disturbance, the percentage of Circulation to Deposits has been much more uniform the one being in closer agreement with the other, than the percentage of Circulation to Capital.

Following is the table of calculations exhibiting this assumed cause and effect, whose showing certainly does not bear the appearance of a mere coincidence of figures :

YEAR.		Excess of Imports over Exports. Per Head of Population.	PERCENTAGE OF BANK CIRCULATION TO		YEAR.	
			Capital.	Deposits.		
			27.4	25.3	1868,	June 30
			26.	20.8	1869	"
June 30,	1868	$ 4 71	44.2	28.	1870	"
"	1869	2 91	50.4	32.9	1871	"
"	1870	37	55.5	38.7	1872	"
"	1871	6 23	53.6	42.8	1873	"
"	1872	7 98	44.	33.7	1874	"
"	1873	10 41	33.	27.8	1875	"
"	1874	10 16	30.2	27.2	1876	"
"	1875	11 62	28.6	25.6	1877	"
"	1876	3 10	30.5	27.	1878	"
"	1877	5 85	28.2	25.3	1879	"
"	1878	3 38	33.3	23.8	1880	"
"	1879	2 53	44.	27.7	1881	"
"	1880	0 31*	54.9	28.3	1882	"
"	1881	1 62	52.5	30.	1883	"
"	1882	3 90	48.3	27.8	1884	"
"	1883	7 57	48.	28.4	1885	"
"	1884	5 43	47.2	25.8	1886	"
"	1885	4 20	50.	26.6	1887	"
"	1886	4 00	53.5	28.	1888	March 31

* Excess of Exports.

A consideration of the large place occupied by trade discounts and advances among the assets of the Canadian banks, of the state of affairs in general produced by the prevailing commercial system, and a reference to Columns Three and Four of our Analysis, which show in what a degree the maintenance of the Rest and the non-impairment of the Capital of the banks is dependent on the non-depreciation in value of the trade securities they hold, ought to make hesitate those among us who are agitating for a sudden reversal of our present commercial policy, a change which, if effected without due preparation extending over years, must, in throwing down a barrier

against the inflow of foreign manufactures and natural products, administer
a check to the growth of many Canadian industries. However beneficial to
Canada as developing her great natural resources might be the effect of
reciprocal Free-trade with the States in the natural products of each
country—and that it would ultimately be beneficial is not denied,—no
one of experience in business affairs can doubt that the opening of the
Canadian markets to the free sale of American manufactures and imports
—to the surpluses of goods that American manufacturers and importers,
supplying sixty million consumers, could usually afford to sell much
below cost abroad, if by that means they could maintain the price of
the bulk in the home market, securing besides a convenient outlet
in a near foreign market for all such surpluses, — would, to say
the least, disturb commercial values here and endanger investments in
factories and plants. And if any depreciation in the values of commodities or
fixed investments—however partial its scope or brief its duration—should
take place, the shock to general credit, for the effect could not be confined
to the particular interests involved, would be so heavy, that, from the nature
and extent of the interest of the banks, enormous and in some cases perhaps irreparable injury must inevitably result to them.

A Secured Circulation.

IT is difficult to see how, in view of the small proportion of the assets of
the Canadian banks held in investment securities, a natural condition
in a young commercial country, they can be required, as is sometimes
suggested, to deposit Government bonds as security for the redemption of
their Circulation. For they have no funds available for investment in bonds.
In most cases no part of the Reserves could be spared ; the only source from
which the funds could possibly be provided are the Loans and Discounts to
Municipal and other Corporations (amounting to 19 million dollars), Call
and Short Loans, and other Loans and Discounts to the public. But is it
advisable, supposing it possible, to withdraw the large sum necessary to cover
the Circulation with Government from municipal uses and the commerce of
the country ?

The idea of a Government Bond security for Circulation is borrowed
from the National bank system of the United States, in which it is inherent.
But the National bank system is a peculiarity—distinctly a product of the
financial necessities of the civil war, just as the establishment throughout the
whole Western world of a mono-metallic standard was a war measure of Lord
Liverpool's. The purpose of the provision requiring National banks to
deposit Government bonds to cover their Circulation was, not to provide a
guarantee for the redemption of the Circulation, but to provide a market for

Government bonds. It was a measure passed in the stress of war, to sell the bonds of the Government, not to secure the Circulation of the banks ; and perhaps its sole effect for good has been that, on the strength of the security afforded, the National bank notes are current at a uniform value throughout all the States.

Another effect of this particular feature of the National bank system has been what might have been expected from acting on the principle of regulating the amount of credit Circulation—purely an affair of trade—by so unconnected a thing as the volume of the National Debt ; for that is what the Act does. No inconvenience was felt at first, while the Debt was sufficiently large to afford a satisfactory basis for the amount of bank Circulation needed in trade ; but as the Debt diminished and bonds were redeemed, the horizon of the banking world grew dark and troublous ; and Mr. Flannagan tells us in his paper, that, whereas in 1866 the amount of bank Circulation was $215 million dollars (and in 1879, 300 million), in 1887, by reason of the reduction of the Debt, the Circulation had been reduced to 169 million ; while, on the other hand, the Deposits had increased since 1866 by 150 per cent.

With the reduction of the Debt, indeed, the bank Circulation has come to occupy a quite subordinate place in the national currency ; and but a very insufficient substitute for it has been supplied in a larger store of gold and silver bullion, whose use, however, as a distinct retrogression, is quite unsuited to the habits of the American people : and this is clearly shown, while the truth of Mr. Flannagan's contention that the diminished quantity of bank Circulation is not sufficient for the business requirements of the country is incidentally proved, by the singular eagerness with which an issue of silver certificates has been absorbed by the public—52 million dollars worth (in ones, twos, and fives) having gone into circulation within 17 months.

With the extinction of the Debt, the *raison d'être* of this security provision, as indeed of the National bank system itself, will cease. It is questionable if the National bank system, at least in its present shape, will survive the Debt. Already the older and freer system of State banks (whose Circulation has been taxed out of existence in order to foster the National bank system), being more accordant with the genius and political habit of the American people, is reviving and making its way again in the world, notwithstanding the disadvantages of mere local credit and difficulty in exchanges that must necessarily attend the operations of the banks of thirty-eight several States mostly dissimilar in laws.

An attempt may be made to preserve the security feature of the National bank system by permitting the substitution of other securities for Government bonds ; but it is doubtful if that be feasible or if it would be convenient and sufficient ; for it were a troublesome task to both banks and Government to keep the new securities, of many descriptions and fluctuating values, nicely adjusted so as to cover, and not more than cover, the amount required by law.

The Circulation of the Canadian banks is already very well secured by being made a preferential charge on all the assets ; and no loss can now likely accrue to any noteholder by failure, unless he be compelled by necessity to part with his notes before sufficient assets can be realised to redeem them. That has been felt as a hardship ; and if it be thought necessary and a point of good policy to prevent it, this may perhaps be done without disturbance to the existing system by some such means as the taking by Government of a statutory lien on the first realised assets, on the investments representing Rest, if separate, on the security attaching to the Double Liability, or on any similar resources ; and then, on the failure of a bank, redeeming its Circulation forthwith. The Government would thus be amply secured, and much suffering might be spared innocent noteholders ; but the difficulty here is that some reserve fund must be provided, available at short notice, to meet any such contingent demand.

On the whole, there seems to be no inducement to transplant this exotic of a National bank system into Canada ; and to engraft its security feature —a matter of mere local expediency—on the Canadian system, would be both inexpedient and without reason, for the circumstances of banking in Canada are quite different.

GOVERNMENT OR BANK CURRENCY?

WE hear it proposed that the Canadian banks shall be deprived of the right to issue Circulation ; that the right of issue shall be vested in Government alone, who shall issue a " National" currency in exchange for and interchangeable with Government bonds, or in payment for public works as they progress, or on some such basis. But for any Government to attempt to so monopolise the currency of a country by a purely Government paper issue, in an arbitrary volume, at the will or according to the needs of Government and without respect to the needs of commerce, would be to mistake the functions of Government : what might come of it may be seen in the case of the Russian paper rouble, which, partly it is true from the fall in the price of silver, but chiefly from having been over-issued by way of Government loans, is to-day worth little more than one third its nominal amount. Such errors in finance must always end in mischief or disaster. That was the case in France with her *assignats*, and in the United States with their continental money. A vast amount of Debt for which no value was given was incurred during the four years of the American civil war, and great disturbance of values took place, owing to the depreciation of the greenbacks issued by the Government after the suspension of specie payments in 1861 ; which, because issued in quantity necessary to carry on the war without respect to the commercial needs of the country, rapidly declined in purchasing power, prices of everything Government had to buy, including gold, as rapidly rising. Government issues, indeed, while arbitrary in volume cannot be suitable to the requirements of commerce : in the most favorable circumstances they will be rigid in amount where they ought to be expansive, and usually will exceed or fall short of the quantity actually needed.

In general, it may be said, the less legal-tender money there is, with a forced circulation, the better. A commercial people requires an expansive credit-money, flowing naturally and as a consequence from commercial transactions and circulating by the free will of the people, and while not absolutely equivalent to gold yet sufficiently supported by a gold reserve. For gold must for safety sake be behind every paper currency as well as ultimately behind every bargain in trade. Such and so supported is our present bank Circulation ; which, moreover, in point of elasticity is a highly efficient commercial currency, partaking more of the nature of bills of exchange, or the cheques of individuals, than of legal-tender money. On the other hand, the futility of attempting to circulate Government legal-tender paper money in a commercial country, otherwise than to meet the demands of commerce and through the proper commercial channels, may be seen by the fate of the Dominion note issue, two-thirds of which is constantly held by the banks in their vaults as Reserves. As Reserves these notes are an eminent success, supplying the place of gold to the banks and saving by their use the interest on so much gold to the country. But they fail as a currency, except as respects the small notes used as change,—a failure that, however, is only in obedience to the natural law under which a cheap money always drives a dearer one out of use, and a credit-paper money drives out coin.

" A Government ' promise to pay,' as Mr. Flannagan says, " may and has been unconstitutionally given the function of money [in the States] by being clothed by statute with the legal-tender quality ;" but any such issue, there or here, being based, not on any form of property, but by a strange anomaly on a National Debt, and not receiving currency through the natural channel of the banks, must be entirely inadequate to the purposes of a commercial currency, and should be limited in amount so as to be only subsidiary to the Circulation proper—that supplied by the banks. The National bank Circulation being issued only against the deposit of Government bonds, although not legal-tender, is essentially a Government currency. It is in consequence wanting in fluent quality and adaptability to local requirements. Lately, in parts of United States territory contiguous to the Canadian border, especially in Maine, the notes of Canadian banks have been a chief circulating medium, because by the operation of the National bank system an excess of currency is caused in the neighborhood of cities where banks are clustered in plenty, and a deficiency where they are few or of small capital—as in these border districts, which naturally need more instead of less currency than city neighborhoods on account of the lack of facilities for doing business by means of token-money—checks, drafts, etc. Hence the late attempted taxation of Canadian bank notes, notwithstanding that manifestly the National bank Circulation is inadequate to the business done in such districts as these.

Government being outside of and unconnected with the sphere of commerce, cannot with advantage to commerce assume one of the functions of banking unless it assumes all. This was clearly recognised many years ago by both British and American Commissions on the currency. The Hon. Willis S. Paine, Superintendent of the Banking Department of the State of New York, says in his report for last year :—"The advocates of a fixed Governmental issue of circulating notes in preference to that of banks seem to forget that as the business of the Government is distinct from that of the mercantile community, it cannot well carry on that portion of the business of banking unless it undertakes all of that business, for the reason that Circulation is needed in proportion to the amount of credit required ; circulating notes are simply credits in a negotiable form.". "A bank circulation is a necessity," says Mr. Flannagan further, "unless the Government undertakes, either through a Government bank, or by some other mode yet to be ascertained, to grant commercial credits. The relation between the Circulation and commercial credits is so intimate that if the Government assumes such control of the former as to practically prohibit its issue, it necessarily limits the latter." The main stream of Circulation must, in fact, in any commercial country flow from the public Deposits, making current so much of their amount as is needed to carry on the minor operations of business. That practically is what takes place in the great monetary centres of Europe. The French and the German Governments, it is true, control the paper Circulation of France and of Germany, but they do it only through the Banks of France and Germany, which each grants credits and issues notes, not at the will of the Government, but in response to the demands of commerce. The Bank of England does the same, maintaining the most intimate terms with the commercial world ; and though part of its note Circulation, being issued against Debt due to the Bank by Government, may be considered a Government currency, Government is kept at arm's length by the whole currency being dealt with through a separate Issue Department.

Apart from the objection that all plans for a Government currency in

Canada take little or no account of the true principle—the supply of a commercial demand—on which alone a paper currency should be issued, it is difficult again to see how, things being as they are, the Canadian banks can be required to withdraw their discounts and advances to the public to so great an extent as the amount of their present Circulation. That is what such proposals involve, and the thing is quite impossible in the circumstances ; while, on the other hand, in putting into circulation, as the banks do, as much of their Deposits as is required for the accommodation of trade, they but fulfil a legitimate function of banking, that ought not to be interfered with by Government. Government has already invaded one province of banking, and so sensibly contributed to the high rates of interest prevailing, in establishing the Post-office and Government Savings Banks, through which the large sum of 40 million dollars of the working capital of a comparatively poor commercial people—equal to more than one-third the total Deposits held by the banks—has been injuriously diverted from commerce, from aiding in developing the resources of the country. But such a violation of economic principle, tolerated though it may be in England, where is an over-abundance of realised wealth, is not to be excused, much less extended in practice, in Canada, where more, not less, capital than we have is needed in commerce.

The Canadian bank Circulation is practically the whole paper currency of the country (the Dominion notes current, to the amount of about 5 million dollars in small denominations, being used only as change); and this state of the currency, sanctioned by long usage, is a natural circumstance of the condition of the country, the course of whose fiscal policy and development of whose banking system has not, like that of the States, been disturbed by the necessities of a nation at war. That this Circulation is and has been a suitable one and of very great utility, free as a whole from the taint of inflation, which, indeed, is impossible with it as a whole, is clearly shown by the absence of any violent spasms or crises in the home money market, or marked fluctuations in the prices of commodities, and the generally uniform rates of interest ; for if the rate of interest has at times been high, that has been caused, in its origin, by over-importations and a consequent low state of the Reserves, a scarcity resulting of course in dearness of money.

There is no better banking system than the Scotch—a system that has aided immensely in the development of the agricultural and mercantile interests of Scotland, while the banks themselves have benefited equally, through being constantly adapted to local and contemporaneous circumstances. A distinguishing feature of that system has always been the granting of cash-credits, resting on bank Circulation, without which indeed the credits would have been impossible in the poor circumstances of the country ; and to this is directly due so flourishing a state of Scotch industries and so great a development of the resources of the country, that the principle involved in Sir Robert Peel's Acts of 1844-5, the substitution of the legal-tender issue of the Bank of England and of specie for the present bank Circulation, is now regarded as adoptable, or at any rate as the development towards which Scotch banking must approach when it next moves. But without the beneficial nursing the industries and resources of Scotland have enjoyed for a hundred and sixty years by means of these bank credits afforded by the use of bank Circulation—the only way, I repeat, such aid could have been rendered—no such progress could have been made, and no such end would be in sight.

Such an end is to be kept in sight in Canada also; but Canada is to-day at much the same stage of fiscal and industrial development that Scotland was in the earlier days of her banking system, when, like Canada now, she most needed its aid; and it can only be after a similar nursing of Canadian resources under a native banking system, that has its counterpart to the Scotch cash-credits in the lines of discount granted to traders, with the use of an elastic bank Circulation, that Canada can hope to reach an equally good position.

THE RIVAL MONETARY STANDARDS.

ALTHOUGH a consideration of the universal standard question does not properly lie within the scope of this paper, yet perhaps it may be useful to trace its salient features in rough outline, in order that the position of Canada in the currency question may be the better understood.

In brief, then, we have before us a world whose ancient and customary currency, as far as civilisation has extended, has always been silver. But in the early part of this century, that condition was disturbed by England, who then, for the first time in history, set up gold as the Western standard of value; and this measure being followed by a policy of Free-trade, which gave her the advantage of a start in business over every other nation, all of whom she forestalled by investing largely in foreign markets when stocks were cheap, England soon became the banker of modern Europe, reaping an enormous harvest from her investments, as the first in the field usually does, and becoming the creditor-nation of the whole world. The debts due her being stipulated to be paid in gold, it has fallen out that this one of the precious metals, a commodity that England owns most of, alone of all commodities in general use has not depreciated in value, doubtless chiefly because it cannot be produced in any considerable quantity or by cheaper methods—a circumstance that, with its convenient bulk, gives it an unrivalled utility as a permanent debt-paying instrument—and in part perhaps through having been given an added importance by being made a principal standard of value. So that, while during the past few years all other commodities, including the other precious metal, silver, have from a cheapening in cost of production (in the case of silver from having been demonetised also) depreciated some 30 per cent. in value, gold has if anything rather appreciated ; and thus the hundreds of millions of foreign gold-bonds owned by England have had near a third added to their value, while the thousands of millions of gold securities owned by the great army of mortgagees, bond-holders, debenture-holders, bank, loan, and insurance company shareholders, have increased by as much, in as far at least as their funds have been kept invested in gold securities. And on the other hand the debtor-classes—the people who owe this money, the landlords, the farmers, the manufacturers, in England, as well as the wheat, beef, cotton, and produce grower abroad, have to give one-third more of their produce than they did fifteen years ago, to liquida e an equal amount of indebtedness for principal or interest.

Still, this disturbance is only local to the Western world. In the far East, where the improvements in methods of production and distribution that have revolutionised prices in the West are for the most part yet unheard of, the old range of prices still prevails in all domestic trade, and silver serenely reigns supreme, its purchasing power quite unaffected by the fall in its price elsewhere. And the reason is, because, great as has been its production in the West, sufficient to force down its price there, where it is merely a commodity, it has not yet been and probably never can be imported into India, China, and the East generally, where it is not merely a commodity, but the currency in use by 800 million people, in quantity sufficient to appreciably disturb current values. If, indeed, silver were poured into these countries (which could only be done, however, in exchange for exportable commodities, a process to which there is a visible limit), the people would grow richer of course, but not much effect would probably be produced on the currency ; for, following the habit engendered by centuries of insecurity, the extra wealth would be hoarded. No serious monetary disturbance, indeed, is likely to take place in the East unless silver should be produced in such over-abundance as to cause a dislocation of its value there and the value of other commodities, similar in extent, though reverse in direction, to the dislocation in the relative values of gold and other commodities in the West. It is only when silver has to be exported from the East to pay gold debts in Europe that this currency experiences a depreciation : Indian civil servants and other Europeans paid in silver who have to remit money to Europe lose a third of their income in doing so ; and so with gold investments in banks and commercial establishments in the East, in as far as their investments are now represented by securities payable in the currency of the

East they have depreciated in value, to the European owner, to the same extent.

But, on the other hand, the depreciation of silver in the West with increased transit facilities and cheaper ocean freight have vastly stimulated Eastern foreign trade, because the lower prices obtained for produce in the European markets are compensated for by a correspondingly increased quantity of silver obtained in exchange ; so that practically the East, while using a silver currency maintaining its value for internal trade and yet at a discount abroad, does not suffer from the prevailing low range of produce prices.

Very different, however, is it with this continent. Here the domestic currency is on a gold basis ; and the agricultural producer is not enabled, like the Asiatic, to obtain an increased quantity of currency to compensate him for the fall in the value of his produce. He sells for gold at the reduced prices prevailing, and no compensating source of profit being available, he has to give an increased quantity of produce to liquidate his indebtedness to the creditor-classes—the moneyed institutions of the Eastern States chiefly, which as gold owners occupy much the same position towards this continent that England does towards the world. Nevertheless, despite this disadvantage as compared with the Indian wheat-grower, the American agriculturist is able to make headway, because from the extension of railway facilities, the cheapening of freights, and the improvements in agricultural implements and labor-saving methods, the saving effected of late years in the cost of American wheat laid down in England is greater than the total amount of the depreciation in price, enormous as that has been.

Thus we see the Eastern world separated from the Western—and as respects India, the British Empire cut in twain—by a line of fiscal cleavage of Britain's own creation. Through this, however, the trade and productive resources of India have been developed enormously of late ; while, on the other hand, it is doubtful if the check that would be administered to the industrial progress of the East by the reverse step of remonetising silver in the West, would at all correspondingly benefit the agricultural interest of this continent. For though with the appreciation of silver the present premium to Indian exporters would disappear, all that could be gained by the American exporter would be the disappearance of one competitor out of several in the British markets ; and that competition had better be met by further improved business methods.

But as respects Canada particularly—who is interested in this silver question, not like the United States as a producer or a user of silver, but only as an agricultural country and another competitor in wheat-growing with India,—it is certain that, occupying a quite subordinate place in the financial world, no other course is open to her than to follow others, making the best of the situation she finds herself in, while going whither she is led. There is no panacea at hand for the trouble of low prices : seventy cents worth of either wheat or silver cannot be made worth a dollar by simply marking it as worth that.   But a manifest duty that lies at our statesmen's hands is, besides promoting every means of cheap transport to enable Canada to compete successfully with India in the English markets, to maintain the currency on so sound a basis as not at any rate to impede the development of trade.   And that end will not be attained by a forced issue of Government paper, or by hampering the banks and the commerce of the country by causing the withdrawal of a further thirty million dollars from trade for investment in Government bonds.   To increase the volume of Canadian exports, it cannot be too strongly urged, is an end to be kept steadily in view : our exports must be made to cover our imports ; and this can be done best with an elastic currency free from redundancy on the one hand, which tends to artificially raise prices above the exporting point, or from deficiency on the other, which equally disturbs trade by lowering prices and so discouraging speculation.

For near twenty years, England, while engaged in her terrible struggle with Napoleon, carried on all her home industries successfully on a paper currency, producing sufficient to pay for all her imports and to yield a balance of gold in her favor ; and the attainment of a similar result in Canada, while all-important in the struggle with competition, is surely as possible in our circumstances.   It is essential, however, that perfect confidence be felt in the currency—a good, probably the sole good, that would be conferred with the legal-tender quality.   It is also desirable that it pass current without discount everywhere in Canada; but this advantage, though urged as a principal reason for a national currency, is hardly of sufficient weight to counterbalance the consideration that legal-tender money is generally unsuitable to a commercial people : while neither cheques and other bills of exchange, nor gold and silver coin, can be sent free of expense from one end of Canada to the other, why should the currency, which is simply one of the convenient substitutes for coin ?

Such a currency, I conclude, bearing a constant ratio in volume to the volume of trade, can best be procured by the natural process of issuing it through the banks ; and only, I am persuaded, through the export trade that will be fostered by a suitable currency can the fund of bank Deposits be largely increased, the investments already made in Canadian industries be strengthened, and a solid available Reserve of gold equivalents be accumulated in greater abundance in our banks.

GOVERNMENT BANK INSPECTION.

AS banks of issue supplying practically the sole currency in use by the people, who thus become from habit often involuntarily, and indeed unknowingly, creditors of the banks whose bills they receive, the Canadian banks might reasonably, perhaps, be required to submit to some degree of Government supervision in respect of their Circulation. But full Government inspection, as generally understood and occasionally advocated in Canada, is again an idea taken from the States, where it was instituted with the establishment of the National bank system, not, however, in order that a Government supervision over the general business of the banks should be exercised, but to ensure the carrying out of certain provisions of the Bank Act—respecting the holding of real estate, loans on which, as in Canada, are prohibited; the limitation of the amount of loans to any one borrower; and the keeping of a sufficient Reserve. Afterward, this inspection, apparently proving a useful check, grew into favor, until the public, coming in time to regard the National banks as in some sort Government institutions, national in everything as well as in name, came also to look to Government to supervise and control the conduct and policy of the bank officials; which it did; and so well did the performance of this extra function recommend it, that a similar provision has been adopted by a few of the States in respect of State banks, mortgage, loan, and guarantee companies, and other private corporations, together with the county treasuries and other public offices, all of whose accounts are regularly inspected by State examiners.

Doubtless, owing to the great number of banks in the States, where a bank may be organised and set in operation on a capital of a few thousand dollars only, some degree of Government supervision is there necessary. Possibly also, the United States system of bank inspection may have done good; the knowledge that speedy exposure must follow wrong-doing might sometimes act as a wholesome deterrent, preventing wrong-doing; though from the many banks that have failed disastrously soon after undergoing successfully the ordeal of an examination, it is evident this safeguard is very inefficient. But however that be, is it advisable to transplant the system here, where the conditions of banking are very different, and where its chief function as now understood, to ensure the proper conduct of the affairs of private corporations, is not usually considered the business of Government? This function surely savors too much of paternal Government, and can be little agreeable to the taste and habits of our people, who usually wish above all things for freedom from Government interference in private trading. The complaint is not unheard in the States that appointments to the office of bank examiner are made sometimes—rarely, it is to be hoped—not because the appointees are competent bank examiners and accountants, but because they have been useful politicians; which is a danger not to be lost sight of even in Canada.   It cannot be considered the duty of Government to prevent dishonesty among bank officials ; that, according to Canadian ideas, is the duty of the Directors. Moreover, a Government guardianship is apt to lull those concerned into a security that can safely be indulged in only in reward for the constant exercise of individual caution and watchfulness, and may thus work positive harm instead of good, if it cause shareholders to cease to maintain the lively interest in their affairs essential to continued success.   And, finally, if Government Bank Inspection be introduced into Canada, it must be after the pattern of the State laws, not the National bank Acts, so as to include in its operation every loan or other company receiving Deposits ; for otherwise the ostensible purpose of protecting the people will not be fulfilled.

There is reason, no doubt, in the contention that Government should have power to satisfy itself that the provision of the Bank Act sanctioning the issue of Circulation has not been contravened by over-issues, that the Capital of the banks has not been impaired by bad investments, in order to assure the noteholders.   But this result may be attained otherwise than by so radical a measure as Government bank inspection : if Government required Bank Returns and Statements to be certified by professional auditors, a sufficient assurance would be afforded noteholders. As between the banks and their depositors no good reason can be given for Government intervention : depositors entrust their money to the banks voluntarily, in open day ; it is a mutually free transaction between both parties ; and therefore with that Government has no right to interfere.   And it surely is not the business of Government to interfere between the shareholders and their executive officers, which appears to be the sole other possible ground for action.

PROFESSIONAL AUDIT.

THE system of inspection now in use in Canadian banks serves merely as a check by the Management on the internal economy of the banks and the operations of the branches.   It leaves the operations of the Management itself untouched, and affords no assurance whatever to the shareholders or the public that the affairs of the bank as a whole are properly conducted.   In every one of the more important cases of bank mismanagement or failure that have occurred in Canada of late years, while the business was shown to have been regularly inspected by the appointed officials, little or nothing of the trouble was in any case divulged outside the bank walls—till disaster did it.

In view of this repeated warning, it is somewhat remarkable that bank shareholders, partners in the most considerable business concerns of the

country, have not long ago perceived the necessity and advantage of applying to those concerns a rule that I suppose every one among them of any
business experience applies to the pettiest of other corporate affairs he has to
do with. From these, as a matter of course, he requires the assurance of
the true condition of their affairs afforded by an audit independent of the
Management: then why not the same from banks? If when the Management
and the Directorate rendered an account of their stewardship to the
shareholders, these received it through one—whether appointed by Management, Directorate, or Shareholders, is not important—whose particular
business it was to deal with accounts, and whose duty it was as Auditor to
"listen," as it has been happily expressed, not with the ears of the Management or of the Directorate, but of the Shareholders, an assurance would be
conveyed of the correctness of the accounts that is wholly lacking now.

There is no real obstacle to a sufficient audit of the affairs of a bank. The
number of the branches in most cases may be thought to be one : in the
States, banks have no branches, each bank's business being contained within
its four walls, which is held to account for the feasibility of Government
bank inspection there, and, by parity of reasoning, to show that where the
business is spread among many branches Inspection or Audit is difficult or
impossible. But auditing is universally practised in England, by statutory
requirement, and there several of the banks have many more branches than
have Canadian banks. The London and County Bank, for instance, has
167 ; yet we find the annual statement of its affairs to be certified by two
professional auditors, who declare that they have "examined the balance-
sheet and profit and loss account, and verified the cash balance at the Bank
of England, the stocks there registered, and the other investments of the
Bank." They have also "examined the several books and vouchers showing
the cash balances, bills, and other amounts set forth," the whole of which
they declare are correctly stated ; and they are of opinion that the balance-
sheet and profit and loss account "are full and fair, properly drawn up, and
exhibit a true and correct view of the Company's affairs as shown by the
books of the Company." The last quoted clause is the auditor's certificate
required under "The Companies' Act 1879 ; " and surely as much as that at
least could be required in Canada.

In Australia also, where the banks have also many more branches than
the Canadian banks, professional auditors are employed ; we find the
annual report of the Commercial Banking Company of Sydney certified to by
two auditors, who say they have "examined the securities, compared the
balances, and counted the coin," which they find as specified on the balance-
sheet. And in China even, a similar practice is in use ; the last statement
of the Hong Kong and Shanghai Banking Corporation has appended the

certificate of two auditors, who say they have "compared the above statements with the books, vouchers, and securities at the head office, and with the returns from the various branches and agencies," finding all correct.

What is being done elsewhere may be done in Canada. Unquestionably, a bank statement, equally with a statement of the affairs of any other corporation, ought to be attested by a competent auditor, one in this case familiar with the theory and practice of banking, besides being an expert accountant, who would be independent of the bank, and whose professional reputation would be at stake in his work. A competent and discreet man so qualified, knowing exactly what particulars of the business were essential to a sufficient audit, would be able to select these for examination without needless intrusion elsewhere. An audit though partial may be perfect so far as it goes, and fully answer the purpose intended. The auditor need not necessarily go minutely into every detail of the business : there must be a limit to investigation if practical work is to go on. An accountant cannot be perpetually testing the accuracy of his Interest Tables : he must, if he is to get his work done, place some degree of faith in their statements ; and in like manner an auditor, when he examines the accounts of a factory or a warehouse does not usually " take stock " himself, but is content to rely on the correctness of the stock-sheets signed by the persons in charge or cognizant of the facts. Surely he can put the same measure of faith in a banker or a merchant that he puts in a mechanic ; and so in a bank audit he may usually rely for much on certificates or statements signed by more than one officer or a committee of Directors.

He might also be able to render good service to the institution by directing attention to any dangerous, yet unsuspected, tendencies in practice, which a trained and fresh mind from outside would be quick to perceive ; and a more ostensible advantage of his employment would be that by it much current hostile criticism would be disarmed, and the popular feeling that seems always to run against banks might be stemmed. This feeling, sometimes righteous perhaps in its origin, though unreasoning in its application, cannot otherwise fail in the long run to be prejudicial to every bank : it is the root of the cry for Government Bank Inspection and Government Security —demands the like of which are far from men's thoughts in England because auditing has been there brought to so great perfection and its practice is so general, that no other safeguard is felt to be needed.

A professional audit, indeed, on a clear survey of the whole field we have traversed forcibly suggests itself as a chief thing wanting in the Canadian banking system—a desideratum that, if adopted, would, as nothing else could, convince the public that whatever might be amiss in that system would be rectified, and ensure that the practice of Canadian banking should always be equal to the really great goodness of its theory.

I HAVE done. If I cannot say also *c'est fini*—if my undertaking cannot be considered as at all a finished performance, even within its limits, I beg it to be remembered that the subject is a wide one, on which few perhaps could say the last word as well as the first. At any rate, all cannot well be said at once. What I have been able to accomplish, however, I now most willingly submit to the criticism of the profession, of bankers, and of publicists, that it may receive the correction and enlargement, the improvement and fuller illustration, that the product of any one mind cannot fail to receive from the richer and more varied experiences of many others. My desire has been to arrive at the truth—not to urge any particular theory or view of my own. I have endeavored to state the case plainly and as concisely as possible, in a business-like way and without rhetoric—a mode of treatment which may sometimes have the appearance of dogmatism ; but I have no wish to speak dogmatically ; on the contrary, I invite criticism and correction, and shall be grateful for any such furtherance to the common object we all have in view.

There are aspects of the subject with which I have not dealt : upon such points of the Returns, for instance, as lay outside the scope of my argument, or that I thought called for no comment, I have made none. So far as I have gone, however, I trust I have treated the subject with candor and without prejudice : my concern has been with a system, not with particular instances of its operation ; and while pointing out the purport, as it appeared to me, of the several features of the Returns, I have, as will have been observed, carefully refrained from applying any of the tests supplied by the Analysis, it might be invidiously, to any particular institution. That I consider outside the province of this paper.

I had no purpose to serve in undertaking this task beyond the ascertainment of the fitness of the principles that seem to lie at the foundation of the Canadian banking system, and the illumination of a subject that is evidently obscure to many people. In dealing with it, however, I venture to think that I have been able to furnish a something that may at least serve as a help to a more scientific framing of the Bank Returns, for the better information of the public ; and perhaps as material for the amendment of the Bank Act in the direction of a new constructive policy in some departments of banking.

The Canadian banking system has been developed to its present stage by progressive changes in the commercial condition of the country, growing with the growth of the country, and being constantly adapted to new wants as they arose. In this lies its great strength and value, that it is not a symmetrically finished system incapable of alteration, imposed from without, but a native of the soil, capable of further growth in any direction it may be

desired to train it.   Upon Parliament rests the duty of periodically recon-
sidering the condition of this system—of seeing that it keeps pace in development with the progress of the country, and is constantly kept adjusted
to all new needs of a growing commerce.   And it is of the utmost importance
that all changes made shall be in accordance with sound economic
principles.

Regard should be had by our legislators rather to the example set by English banking legislation than by American, notwithstanding that the American
system may be thought to be more akin to our own.   For in the United
States, from the day when General Jackson marred an otherwise successful
career by his vengeful and disastrous treatment of the Bank of the United
States, with but few intervals of better treatment the Government has generally failed in its banking legislation, because sound principle has usually
been made to give way, in that as in other legislation, to political expediency.
While, on the other hand, in England, the remarkable success that attended
the introduction and after-development of all Sir Robert Peel's fiscal policy,
due to his grounding it on the best theoretical knowledge of his day, is
eminently conspicuous in the enduring character of his banking legislation,
which has successfully passed through the trying ordeal of a sheer revolution
in values and business methods—not confined to one country but world-
wide—brought about by improvements in methods of production and increased facilities of distribution and business communication.   And it is
hard to conceive of higher praise of any fiscal policy than the praise that may
be justly accorded to this, which in the midst of so shifting a scene, has stood
firm for more than forty years, scarcely needing the smallest revision.

Let us hope Canadian statesmen, building upon an equally sure foundation, may be able to carry the structure of Canadian banking to as high a
pitch of excellence.

MEMORANDA

WITH REGARD TO MR. MENZIES' PAPER ON BANKS AND BANKING.

NOTE.—The papers in this appendix were written in reply to the first draft of the treatise; which was revised and the argument amplified before being read.

(1.) In the opening paragraph reference is made to *special knowledge* of the subject. This is most pertinent. There is no subject in which a want of special knowledge is more likely to lead a person astray. Special knowledge should be not merely of sets of figures, but of what lies behind the figures, in the complicated masses of business which they represent.

(2.) It is stated that the limitation of Circulation to Capital is apparently grounded on no principle. This remark is incorrect. Circulation is Credit, taken by a Banker, and given to him by the public. It is a universal principle, well justified by long experience, that *Credit* should be based on *Capital*. To base the circulation of Banks on their capital is therefore rational, and in accordance with the teachings of experience.

(3.) The relations of Circulation to Deposits are evidently entirely misunderstood, both by the writer and by the New York authority whom he quotes. The latter has evidently had no practical experience of Circulation, and neither understands how it arises nor on what it rests. This is not remarkable, seeing that New York Bankers have no experience, properly speaking, of Circulation at all. The Bankers there do not redeem their own notes. Redemption is the keynote of the whole system of a proper Circulation. It is only by the function of *redeeming* notes, day by day, and seeing that other Banks redeem them, that any practical experience in Circulation can be had.

This gentleman apparently knows nothing of the distinction between fixed Deposits and floating Deposits. He evidently does not see also that Circulation and Deposits are rather antagonistic than co-related.

When Bank notes are paid in, Circulation decreases and Deposits increase. When a Deposit is withdrawn, it is withdrawn generally in notes; then Circulation increases but Deposits decrease. Moreover, a large amount of Deposits are of a fixed character. Whatever their origin, they remain stationary, and have no influence whatever upon the moving tide of Circulation, either outward or inward.

* * * * * * * *

(4.) The proposal to base the Circulation on Deposits is unsound in theory, and would be unworkable in practice. Deposits are the debts of a Banker; so are his Circulating notes. To propose that because he is in debt in one direction, therefore he is to get into debt in another direction, without any regard to his capital, is manifestly unsound.

(5.) The Banking Act very properly requires a considerable capital to be paid up, before Circulation can be issued at all. Any person can take Deposits, if the public will trust him; but to issue Circulating bills is a function requiring a careful foundation, strict limitations, and the imposition of reasonable safeguards. Experience tends in the direction of requiring a far larger amount of capital to be paid up, before circulating notes can be issued. This is my own opinion. Otherwise a Bank with a small paid-up capital, say $50,000, might attract twenty times that amount of Deposits by offering high rates of interest. If, then, it could issue a circulation of one-half or one-third of its Deposits, a superstructure of credit would be raised which the least breath would topple over.

But such a proposal would be unworkable in practice. The whole of the current Deposits of a Canadian Bank are the sums flowing out and in, at from ten to thirty places over the whole extent of the Dominion; and the amount is beyond the Banker's control. It would be utterly impossible for him to keep Circulation, which is itself a fluctuating quantity, in regular correspondence with another fluctuating quantity. Such a proposal could only by any possibility be carried out, where the whole business of a Bank was done in one Office.

(6.) With regard to the Rest. The proposal to insist upon Banks investing the amount of their Rest in other securities than discounted bills and trade advances, sounds well, but it is not practical.

A Banker has always out a large line of liabilities which are payable on demand, and others payable at a very short notice. The payment of his liabilities on demand is the foundation principle of his business. The moment that is impaired, a Bank ceases to exist as an active institution. Every consideration, therefore, shows that in any investing or disposing of his assets, the first and fundamental principle to be kept in view is the being able to command resources wherewith to meet his liabilities. If then the Rest were by statutory authority placed beyond his disposal, his power to meet his obligations daily would be imperilled—a position which no Banker would consent to.

The proposal to place such enormous sums of money as are represented· by Bank Rests, in the hands of persons outside the Banks, is really so unbusinesslike that it can hardly be treated seriously. Who are to be the trustees for the Seventeen Millions of money represented by the "Rests" of the Canadian Banks? Is it possible to suppose that the Bank of Montreal would trust any person outside its own circle with the sum of Six Millions ; or that the Merchants Bank of Canada would trust any such person with nearly Two Millions ; or the Bank of Toronto One and a Half Millions? The idea is absurd.

(7.) DOUBLE LIABILITY.—The author of this paper is constantly quoting United States authorities. They have really scarcely any bearing on the Canadian position. Banks there are radically different institutions, founded on different principles, governed by different methods, in many respects far behind the advanced and improved methods current in England, Scotland, and Canada. The little petty institutions, scattered all over the country, dignified by the name of Banks, would not be endured for one moment in Canada.

As to the contingent liability repelling investors, I am not aware that any enquiries have ever been made on the subject. The opinion of the writer is, therefore, based on no foundation.

The writer remarks that Column 3 shows the extent of depreciation in the value of discounted bills that would absorb the Rest.

A practical man—a man with "special knowledge"—would have dwelt largely upon this. In the absence of special knowledge remarks would be dangerous. But it is in one respect the most important column of all.

(8.) EARNING POWER.—The writer's remarks with regard to the Deposits of English and Canadian Banks respectively are worthy of note. But—

1. These remarks have been made repeatedly for the last 20 years in the financial journals, and numbers of illustrations thereof given.

2. The writer does not seem to know the difference between London Banks, which have not and never had a circulation, and the Scotch and Irish Banks, which have a circulation, as well as numbers of the Country Banks of England itself. That the Scotch and English Banks value their circulation is evidenced by the strenuous fight they made for it at the time when Sir Robert Peel proposed to deprive them of it.

3. The statement that the Australian Banks commonly show Deposits of twelve or fifteen-fold the amount of their paid-up capital is a little exaggerated; but the writer is apparently not aware that many of these Australian Banks have their head office in London, England, and receive Deposits there, attracting them by offering higher rates of interest than are current with the purely London Banks.

These Banks will often offer 2 per cent. more for money in London for a time Deposit than a London Bank will. Moreover, the Governments of Australasia are not competitors in the Banking field. It is perfectly true, however, and it has often been referred to in our financial journals, that Australia has vastly more money on Deposit than Canada has.

(9.) The Canadian Banking system, it is said, is peculiarly an edifice of Credit. Why peculiarly? This remark not only fails to be true, but it is the exact *opposite* of the truth : for the author has just been showing that the Canadian Banks take far less Credit from the public than almost any other Banks in the world. In no country in the world is there more Banking *capital* in proportion to Banking credit than in Canada.

The note under the head of Column 7 is a peculiar instance ·of the want of special knowledge. Every Bank has arrangements with regard to certain of its resources, which are an essential element in considering its position. A calculation of these resources would, in some cases, make the Reserves stronger, in others not so good.

(10.) The author is in error in stating that Call Loans, and Loans at short notice, are buried in the Discounted Bills Returns of the Canadian Banks. The greater part of them is under the head of Loans on Stocks and Bonds.

(11.) The author constantly uses the term, "The English Banks" do this, or that, when comparing them with the Canadian Banks—a most misleading use of language, for the English Banks referred to are only the thirteen Joint Stock Banks of London, not including the Bank of England.

Even in London there are large and powerful Banking firms, whose credit and business are on a par with that of the Joint Stock Banks. Moreover, the Bank of England is entirely omitted—a huge omission, certainly—and the whole mass of Banks throughout all England, except London, and the Banks in Scotland and Ireland. These also are not taken into account.

To say, therefore, that the English Banks have Loans of $418,000,000, against Canadian $167,000,000, is so grossly inaccurate that it is astonishing that any sensible man could commit himself to it.

(12.) Some of the remarks under the heading of "The Prevailing Commercial System" show a certain want of acquaintance with the subject. There are times during every year when the remarks of the writer are true and pertinent. There are other periods of the year, and of every year, in which such remarks are entirely beside the mark, as the vast amount of funds advanced by the Banks are in steady process of realization day by day, and in that very liquid shape which the author denies them to be.

The remarks as to the connection between the balance of trade and the Circulation are really only to be compared to the sage observation that the tendency of rivers is to run past great cities. When there is a heavy production of exportable commodities, Bank Circulation flows out in the country and backwoods districts in the purchase of them.

The importing business of a country, immense as it is, gives rise to no Circulation at all. The manufacturing business gives rise to very little. It is the purchase of agricultural and other natural products that gives rise to large Circulation. When these articles go abroad they tend to create a balance in favor of Canada. Whether imports come in, or do not come in as a consequence, has little effect upon Banking Circulation. If the next year's production is large, Circulation will still keep up; if it is small, it will undoubtedly go down, and so it will go on year after year. The table given under this head is a very striking example of *non sequitur.*

(13.) The remarks as to a reversal of our present commercial policy are sound and judicious.

(14.) So also are the general remarks on a secured Circulation. But it is not very likely that Government would consent to become a Trustee for note-holders in the manner proposed.

(15.) GOVERNMENT CURRENCY.—The remarks of the author under this head are generally sound and judicious; but they have been brought before the public on more than one previous occasion, and notably in the replies of Bankers to the questions of a Committee of Parliament, previous to the renewal of Bank Charters in 1871, when the whole subject was exhaustively discussed.

What is said as to the disadvantage of Government Currency is highly appropriate. There are some points of detail, however, which require correction. It is stated that the British, French, and German Governments control the Paper Circulation, by the Banks of England, France, and Germany.

The English Government has no more control over the Bank of England than it has over any other Bank. The limit of the Bank of England Circulation, and every other Bank in Great Britain, is fixed by Act of Parliament. So is the limit of Canadian Bank Circulation.

It is constantly overlooked by those who have no special knowledge of this matter that the whole of the Banks of Scotland have a Circulation; so have the whole of the Banks of Ireland, and a large number of the Banks of England and Wales.

(16.) The remarks made with regard to Government Savings Banks are most sound and judicious, though both these and the following part of the Treatise are marred by the reference again to the unreasonable idea that Circulation should be regulated by Deposits.

(17.) RIVAL MONETARY STANDARDS.—A discussion on this point is interesting in theory, but it has no practical bearing on the Canadian position, so far as legislation is concerned.

Canada has always been on a Gold basis, and it will be a pitiful descent indeed if she ever adopts any other. The United States are indeed in great danger of falling to a Silver Standard, and Canadian Banks require to keep this constantly in view. In fact they do so, often making special arrangements that any Loans or Bills domiciled in the United States shall be payable in gold and not in Currency.

(18.) GOVERNMENT BANK INSPECTION.—The remarks here are also pertinent, and the danger and imperfection of Government Inspection well pointed out.

The difficulty of keeping such a system pure and free from partisan influences would be almost insurmountable. It is not, however, pointed out, as it should be, that the advantages supposed to be secured in the United States by a system of Bank examiners are much exaggerated. It is known that these examinations are often of a perfunctory kind. Repeated instances have shown that a Bank may be in a rotten condition and yet pass an examination, failing disastrously within a few weeks after being certified to as sound and correct by the Government itself. But it is well observed that all arguments drawn from Inspection by Government officials in the United States are entirely inapplicable to Canada, owing to our diversified system of Branches.

(19.) PROFESSIONAL AUDIT.—It is evident that the writer has in view that kind of perfunctory examination of a Bank statement which could be had by examining in the Head Office the general Balance Sheet of a Bank, and checking it by Returns furnished by the Branches. He apparently perceives clearly enough that no other audit is possible. That this is neither an Inspection nor a proper Audit goes without saying. It would amount to nothing except to lull stockholders into a fancied security which really did not exist.

It is generally forgotten by persons unfamiliar with the subject, that a constant audit of a really effective character is going on all the year round in every Canadian Bank, and that the elaborate Returns furnished to the Government have all been prepared on models, the result of years of discussion and experience and that they are examined in a Department of the Government. It is sometimes forgotten, too, that no persons are so deeply interested in the correctness of Bank Returns and Statements as the Directors of a Bank, who, by their very office, must be large stockholders. But most of all it is forgotten that any audit of a Canadian Bank, to be really efficient, must be of a vastly more comprehensive and expensive character than is imagined.

A complete and efficient audit of the position of the Bank of Montreal alone would require the services of a staff of experienced officials, who could not possibly finish the work under six or eight months; indeed, it would be more correct to say, under twelve months, which is as much as to say that it should be perpetual. This staff would require to be within the walls of the Banking Office of the Bank itself during the whole of this time, which is obviously impracticable.

Any other audit than this would, and must, be of a perfunctory character. It would amount to nothing; it would prevent no disaster; it would expose no wrong doing. A Bank could be rotten to the core, yet such an audit would not reveal it, just as examinations in the United States have failed to reveal rottenness. And if the idea of wrong doing and fraud entered into the minds of the higher officers of the Bank, and they desired to conceal the true position, they would smile at the idea of outside professional auditors finding out what was going on, notwithstanding their efforts to conceal it.

The author unconsciously admits the impracticability of a really efficient audit, by stating that in such a one as he proposed he must rely very much on certificates or statements signed by more than one officer, or a committee of Directors. This gives away the whole case. It must *necessarily* be so indeed. But this is exactly what the public have at present, under the terms of the Banking Act.

G. HAGUE.

Montreal, May 14th, 1888.

OBSERVATIONS BY MR. CROSS.

I have had the privilege of watching the growth of this Essay from week to week, and know something of the labor and care bestowed upon it. The attempt is made to deal with principles, and to this end facts have been carefully collected, and their important and necessary features have been faithfully stated; the conclusions offered are confined to those statements. The best feature of the work consists in the honesty which has led the writer to sacrifice his preconceptions when facts have opposed them. This method is entitled to the support of this Institute. We may each find something to dissent from perhaps, but we are placed under an obligation to clearly reveal the grounds upon which we base our dissent, and any additional matter should have the same support. It is not enough that this subject should be understood by Bankers; the more thoroughly the principles are understood by the general public, the better for all concerned. Mystery and ignorance are the only conditions that render panics possible. To no single person is the Canadian public more indebted for his efforts to spread accurate information in this department of National Economy, than to Mr. George Hague. He has often treated the subject as a publicist as well as from a mere Banker's point of view, and upon this account his comments are entitled to all the respectful consideration which they have received.

The proposal to base Circulation on Deposits is doubtless an unworkable one, and Mr. Menzies has not succeeded in showing that it is sound in theory, neither has Mr. Hague shown its unsoundness; there is little difference between fixed and floating Deposits from the moment the former are made active, and the proceeds of the bills discounted are credited to a "floating" account. This *money of account* is the principal medium by which Exchanges are made, and our three classes of Circulation proper are becoming to an ever increasing extent of lesser importance, in fact they acquire their own currency chiefly as change for cheques which themselves are only one form of *money of account*. Many of Mr. Hague's subsequent objections seem to show that the views given are bounded by personal experience, and they illustrate the difference between the Arts and the Sciences. Experience is indispensably necessary to success in the Art of Banking, not so a thorough knowledge of the principles that underlie the Art. The Science of Banking rests upon a broad consideration of the necessities which keep it in existence as an implement of civilization, and the mere experience of any individual cannot furnish these. Indeed the duties of a great trust make such claims upon time and attention that they tend to convert one who would otherwise be an impartial observer into an advocate. This tendency explains the advantage enjoyed by a Board of Directors who are not Bankers in dealing with large questions of policy, though they rarely have the Banking experience of those whom they direct. It has been said that if a proposition in Euclid happened to be adverse to the interests or cherished speculations of a class, arguments would be invented either to confute or to show its inexpediency. If Mr. Hague could spare a little attention to the Scottish or Australian Bank returns, it is probable that he would revise much that he has said, and it may be, withdraw some of the objections made.

The Union Bank of Australia, one of six larger Banks, in 1876 had a reserve of two millions in dollars, and paid a 16% dividend. In 1883 it paid 18%, and had a reserve of over four and a half millions. This reserve having increased at a smaller ratio last year, only 13% dividend was paid. It is obvious that had a 10% dividend been paid during these dozen years and the remainder invested in Government securities, and these deposited with an appropriate State Officer, there would have been a fund in reserve against Shareholders' liability of some five millions of dollars, and the active resources of the Bank would be just what they are to-day.

The Commercial of Sydney, dating from 1834 (three years earlier than, and having only two-fifths the amount of paid-up capital of, the last named), pays 25% on three millions of capital. It has a circulation of nearly five millions and discounts of more than forty millions, yet it has stood the ups and downs of fifty years without "toppling over." It has a reserve one and a quarter times greater than its capital, and holds twelve and a half millions in coin and Government securities. It owes the public sixteen times the amount of its Capital.

A still smaller institution, only 25 years old, The Australian Joint Stock Bank, owes the public fourteen times the amount of its capital. It holds nearly four millions in coin and bullion alone, and over five millions, still speaking in dollars, of convertible securities, pays 12½% dividend, and its rest is nearly 70% of its capital.

Owing to the peculiar position of Canada in being directly connected with two great financial centres, ours cannot, like the Scotch, Irish or Australian Banks, take their cue from London only ; due regard must be, and always has been, had to what is going on in New York. Large metallic reserves are less needed by us, for it is certain that Exchange on those two cities will alone keep our currency on a par with gold so long as the Government shall refrain from competing with the Banking trade. There are many reasons why it should step aside, and it is satisfactory to find from the Finance Minister's remarks on the Savings Banks in his budget speech on 27th ult. that the Government is not unconscious of some of them. It is to be regretted that no data are before us showing the effect of the legal tender issue. The ten millions held by the Banks is made to do national clearing house work on inter-bank settling days, and if it has the effect of saving the country the expense of a gold coinage it is economically expedient that it should be continued. The smallness of the issue has certainly prevented it from interfering with the condition described in that well established axiom of political economists, that "a circulation should vary in amount and value exactly as the currency would do were it metallic."

Sir Robert Peel's Acts, referred to in the final paragraph with approval, had the merits of carefully guarding all existing rights and privileges, and whilst permitting, entirely free banking of framing a few easily understood provisions, affecting Banks of issue. The Act of 1844 limited the privilege of issuing notes to those who then possessed it. That of 1845 enacted that all issues beyond the average about that time must be supported by a reserve of gold coin equal in amount. The minting arrangements were left untouched, otherwise the control of the Circulation was exclusively confirmed to the Banks. Should it appear that our existing banks can do the work, those Acts furnish a precedent for confining the privilege to them. Should provision be made for the deposit with the Auditor or Receiver General of Government Securities for future reserves or any portion thereof as a security in lieu to that extent against double liability, the right of issue should be by that amount enlarged, and in this way a provision would be made for future expansion should its necessity arise.

As to the existing Rests it is obviously unwise that their present employment should be disturbed, but a suggestion founded on the new departure of the present Government with regard to the people's savings may be hazarded. Since the first Act establishing Savings Banks passed the British Parliament in 1817, it has been recognized that such institutions should not be regarded as depositories for *permanent investments*. The State undertakes, on the ground of good policy, to receive the savings of the working classes and to return *money* on demand. The only Chancellor of the Exchequer who ever attempted to depart from this was Mr. Lowe and his proposals were withdrawn. In England, as has been the case in Canada, the State made large losses in interest, but when the Post Office Savings plan was adopted the rate of interest from the first was fixed at 2½ per cent. Our Government have it in their power to make two sound departures simultaneously. They could deposit with each Bank such a portion of these moneys as equalled its actual rest and oblige the Bank to hold Dominion bonds to the amount thereof. This would be more than a mere matter of book-keeping. It would place the onus of providing money for withdrawals upon those whose business it is, and upon whom it would actually devolve were the withdrawals at once large and sudden.

W. H. CROSS, F.C.A.

Toronto, 22nd May, 1888.

REPLY IN SO FAR AS THE PAPER REFERS TO THE ISSUE OF CURRENCY.

Under the heading "Basis of Circulation" our worthy friend states that "the statutory limitation of the Circulation of the banks, to the amount of their unimpaired paid-up Capital, is a purely arbitrary one, apparently grounded on no principle."

I think that there is a principle involved, and a very important one, and that the restriction by law is a very wise one.

If—and I would very strongly emphasize that if—the banks are to be allowed to continue to be banks of issue, they should certainly be restricted in the exercise of this privilege, and I cannot conceive of any index as to the extent of this limitation on any sound principle other than in direct proportion to unimpaired paid-up or accumulated Capital. Surely a bank having an unimpaired paid-up Capital of $10,000,000 may be allowed an issue of ten times that of one with only $1,000,000 of Capital. The business done, and the nature of it, will be the measure of the capacity of any bank to exercise this privilege conferred upon it. No bank, however, any more than any other public company or any private individual, should be able to obtain credit in proportion to the business it wishes to do, or its customers want it to do, without regard to its own Capital invested in the business.

The public have confidence in becoming the creditors of the banks, as holders of the bills in circulation, because of the limitation imposed in restricting issues in proportion to Capital.

If the Capital, Rest, Cash Deposits, and authorized Circulation together fall short of supplying funds for the legitimate wants of the customers of any bank, the same course is open as in the case of other monetary or commercial enterprises, viz., to increase the Capital. If this be not done, the ordinary course of events is that more banks are organized.

The lending of money, especially on personal security, is attended with risk of loss. It is well, therefore, in the interest of the shareholders as well as the public at large, that the expansion of business by way of the issue of currency should be restricted in proportion to Capital.

If this country has not enough of circulating currency it certainly cannot be owing to over-restriction of the issue of the banks by legislation, for we find that the larger banks have not half the issue in circulation which the law allows them, and that of the existing Government issue a large proportion is not in circulation.

As regards, therefore, the amount of the Circulation, there can be only one or other of two conclusions, either we have under the present restriction as much currency as is needed, or else that as yet the source of the issue of our currency is not such as meets the true objects of a circulating medium in providing the true ideal of a thorough and elastic means of substitute for barter.

I have come to the latter conclusion in my mind, whether right or wrong. I am convinced that the Government of a country should take the matter of the issue of currency entirely into its own hands, under wise and comprehensive legislation.

I shall not stop to discuss whether the issue of currency by the Government, instead of banks, would or would not increase the Circulation. I shall not even deal with the question as to whether a larger Circulation is needed in the country or not. I desire rather to point out a system of currency, which, in my opinion, would adjust itself, in an elastic way, to the wants of the people, and solve, in its operation, many vexed questions, which otherwise may well puzzle the most astute and the most experienced to come to any intelligent conclusion.

I am indebted to Mr. Buchanan, of the Dominion Lands' Department at Ottawa, for the suggestion that legal-tender notes issued by the Government to replace bank issues be redeemable on demand in interest-bearing Consols of the Dominion. That these Consols be redeemable on demand in legal-tender currency. The Circulation would thus never be arbitrary in volume but would be perfectly elastic and adjust itself to the requirements of the public.

As regards the details involved in placing such a currency in circulation, it would not be difficult to adjust a suitable scheme.

Of course the banks should be duly considered, and a period of ten or more years given them for the gradual withdrawal of their issues or the equivalent by way of interest paid them by the Government in the event of the immediate assumption by the Government of the entire Circulation.

It is only necessary for the present argument to mention two ways in which the Government could effect such an issue of currency. It might simply supply the banks with all the currency needed under suitable restrictions regarding the respective banks, or it might issue directly a currency in payment for products of the country exporting the same and obtaining gold for it. I am in favor of the latter.

We have a vast wheat-growing district in the North-West. The producers there labor under great disadvantages in disposing of their crops. If the Government of the Dominion should contract for the purchase of the bulk of the wheat grown there, and ship to a foreign market by the Canadian Pacific Railway and its connecting lines, paying therefor both the price and the freight in a new issue of legal-tender Dominion notes, obtaining gold for the products purchased, this might be done year after year until the bank Circulation were entirely replaced. The debenture debt of the Dominion could be redeemed to the amount of such issue, the interest being saved to the Dominion. By redeeming the Circulation by Consols, and redeeming Consols by Circulation, the Government would always save the interest on the amount actually needed in Circulation, but no more and no less. The time would not be far distant when the balance of the Dominion debt, outside of circulating currency, would be owing almost entirely to banks and others in the Dominion, and the demand would be such that our Consols could readily be sold for foreign exchange or in a foreign market at par or its equivalent.

I conceive it to be within the true functions of a Government to encourage in every way practicable the development of the resources of the country. Obviously, if from any cause the banks curtail the advances made to producers or middlemen, the producing or purchasing power in the country is lessened. This may happen concurrently with a good demand in some foreign country for the very commodity sought to be produced or moved. A Government purchasing products of any kind to meet the launching of a direct issue of Government currency would naturally and necessarily be guided by foreign markets as to the nature and extent of such purchases. This power wisely exercised would give a stimulus to the production in the Dominion of commodities in active demand in various parts of the world.

Under the system I have indicated, the amount issued for payment of products need not be restricted to the amounts of the curtailment of bank issues, because, directly the Circulation became inflated beyond need, holders could invest in National funds. On the other hand, if the opportunities of purchase of products did not admit of getting into circulation as much as was needed to replace bank issue, the Government could deposit with the banks the required amount of currency to bear interest at the same rate as was paid on Government Consols.

The instances cited by Mr. Menzies of the issue of National currency have no bearing whatever upon the question of a Dominion of Canada currency such as I have suggested. It would be fruitless to discuss them.

Mr. Menzies' allusion to the existing Government issue is wide of the mark ; the fact is, that these notes being equal to specie in Canada are principally held as such by the banks. If the circulation used by the banks was all of the same nature, a certain amount would naturally be held in the same way.

That the withdrawal of the bank Circulation would be an inconvenience to the public, because of the curtailed power of the banks to make advances, assumes that it is impossible to multiply the numbers of banks, or to increase the capital of those existing, a fallacy which needs no remarks.

In conclusion I would say that if the banks be deprived of their present privilege of issuing circulating currency, the imposition of double liability of stockholders could be abolished as there could then be no pretext for such a law.

I would remark incidentally that if it be deemed expedient to require that bank accounts be audited, the auditors should in my opinion be appointed by the stockholders and not by the Government.

I have endeavored to be very brief in my remarks, but I trust that I have said enough to open up a discussion on one branch of the subject of Mr. Menzies' paper.

WM. POWIS, F.C.A.

Toronto, 15th May, 1888.

POSTSCRIPT BY THE AUTHOR.

On the eve of publication I have received the Banking Supplement issued with the London *Economist* of May 19, from which I learn that eighteen banks in England and Wales, one in the Isle of Man, two in Ireland, and two in Australia hold their Rests, or " Reserves," invested specifically, separate from their other assets. These Rests aggregate 28 million dollars. Chief among the banks so dealing with their Rests are the—

Bank of Ireland.....................................$5,170,000
Union B. of London............................... 4,250,000
Union B. of Australia *............................ 4,287,000
B. of Australasia 2,500,000
Birmingham Joint Stock B........................... 2,149,000
Wilts and Dorset B. Co. 2,000,000
London and Provincial B. 1,548,000
National B. of Ireland............................. 1,157,000
Birmingham B. Co.. 1,146,000

The amount of bank Capital paid up in the United Kingdom is £70 million sterling ; its market value £190 million. The balance of Capital subscribed, callable and reserved, amounts to £170 million ; the Reserve fund, dividends, and undivided profits amount to £34⁷ million. The total amount of Deposits held by all the banks in the United Kingdom, private as well as joint stock, is estimated to be £570 to £580 million.

Of the sixteen Australasian banks, three show Deposits to twelve-fold the amount of their Capital, one to thirteen-fold, and one to fifteen-fold.

ANALYSIS OF BANK STATEMENTS, 31st JANUARY, 1888.

BANKS. (In order of amount of paid-up Capital.)	PERCENTAGE OF						
	Circulation to Capital.	Rest to Capital.	Rest to Disc'nts.	Capital and Rest to Disc'nts.	Capital and Rest to Circulation and Deposits.	Disc'nts to Total Assets.	Cash and Convertible Securities to Circulation and Deposits.
	1	2	3	4	5	6	7
Montreal	44.6	50.	34.7	104.2	78.4	38.1	65.
Commerce	41.3	8.3	3.7	48.6	53.7	66.5	29.9
Merchants'	53.1	29.3	13.7	60.3	66.8	62.7	33.1
British N. America	21.9	22.7	14.2	77.1	85.	62.2	46.
Quebec	27.2	13.	6.1	52.8	57.9	64.5	24.6
Toronto	57.8	62.5	16.8	43.7	49.4	70.7	34.4
Molson's	87.6	43.7	10.5	34.6	36.8	72.2	18.6
Nationale	24.6	....	....	68.2	118.7	71.5	22.3
British Columbia	38.5	25.6	37.7	184.8	91.2	35.2	62.3
Dominion	86.9	71.3	15.9	38.3	33.8	60.5	40.9
Imperial	81.6	36.7	11.7	43.7	33.8	53.5	41.4
Ontario	65.4	35.	10.4	40.1	38.8	64.6	29.6
Eastern Townships	56.9	29.	11.6	51.6	74.5	72.3	15.2
Du Peuple	64.8	20.	5.6	33.6	41.9	80.3	14.9
Union of Canada	70.7	4.2	1.4	35.2	47.9	81.5	7.3
Nova Scotia	100.1	35.9	12.6	47.6	33.	48.9	39.2
Standard	65.3	34.	9.9	38.9	35.9	63.5	34.
Hamilton	93.8	34.	9.9	39.1	43.1	70.	19.6
Ottawa	74.2	31.	11.3	47.6	53.4	64.6	18.6
Merchants' of Halifax	92.8	16.	5.9	42.9	38.4	58.1	40.9
Hochelaga	75.2	14.1	5.7	46.4	56.8	71.9	26.9
People's of Halifax	24.5	7.5	4.8	69.1	110.6	71.5	49.
Traders'	96.	2.	.6	30.8	35.1	75.3	19.5
New Brunswick	85.8	70.	21.2	51.6	48.7	59.9	50.8
Jacques Cartier	82.3	28.	12.	54.9	45.1	52.5	21.4
Halifax Banking Co	99.6	20.	5.2	31.	34.5	78.	13.9
Union of Halifax	29.7	8.	6.1	81.9	82.7	48.5	61.6
Ville Marie	83.2	4.2	2.	49.6	47.5	60.8	11.7
Western	87.1	10.6	3.7	38.8	57.4	70.1	12.
Yarmouth	23.7	10.	5.8	63.6	84.4	64.8	29.5
Commercial of Manitoba	98.2	7.2	2.9	43.7	49.3	68.1	25.9
St. Hyacinthe	64.1	....	....	38.	41.9	71.	18.8
Comm'l of Windsor, N.S.	24.1	25.	17.9	89.6	140.3	59.5	14.7
Exchange of Yarmouth	13.7	12.2	11.6	106.4	419.2	68.5	65.4
St. Jean	20.1	4.4	3.9	91.6	313.9	75.7	18.3
St Stephen's	87.1	12.5	5.6	50.5	87.6	80.6	9.7

LONDON JOINT-STOCK BANK STATEMENTS, 31st DECEMBER, 1887.

BANKS.	PERCENTAGE OF				
	Rest to Capital.	Rest to Discounts and Advances.	Capital and Rest to Discounts and Advances.	Capital and Rest to Deposits.	Cash, Money at Call, and Investments to Deposits.
London & Westminster...	59.4	10.7	28.7	19.7	53.3
London Joint Stock.......	64.7	9.6	24.4	24.	...
Union	50.2	12.3	37.	20.5	62.8
Glyn, Mills, Currie, & Co...	50.	10.	30.	13.3	68.
City	51.4	10.8	31.8	29.9	34.9
Imperial	23.3	6.	31.9	30.7	35.
Alliance	30.6	7.8	33.3	30.6	38.2
Consolidated	28.9	7.9	35.2	29.5	41.8
Central	85.6	11.4	24.7	16.8	46.2
London & South-Western.	19.3	2.9	18.	10.2	43.3
London & County.....	51.1	5.4	16.1	10.3	44.8
Lloyds, Barnetts, & Co......	48.9	5.9	18.	10.5	50.7
London & Provincial.......	91.8	12.8	26.7	16.4	54.5

MEMORANDUM OF TOTALS.

BANKS.	Capital Paid-up.	Rest.	Deposits.	Cash.	Securities.	Advances and Discounts.
36 Canad'n Banks ...	$58,865,000	$17,649,000	$110,513,000	$ 32,356,000	$ 5,960,000	$167,752,000
13 London Banks ...	70,500,000	34,000,000	612,000,000	148,500,000	132,500,000	418,000,000

ANALYSIS OF BANK STATEMENTS, 29th FEBRUARY, 1888.

BANKS. (In order of amount of paid-up Capital.)	PERCENTAGE OF					
	Circulation to Capital.	Circulation to Deposits.	Rest to Capital.	Rest to Disc'nts.	Capital and Rest to Disc'nts.	Cash and Convertible Securities to Circulation and Deposits.
Montreal	45.4	27.	50.	35.9	107.8	63.5
Commerce	39.8	23.1	8.3	3.7	48.5	29.7
Merchants'	53.2	37.9	29.3	13.3	58.6	.31.5
British N. America	22.4	17.4	24.1	15.	77.3	43.2
Quebec	26.2	15.3	13.	6.1	52.7	23.5
Toronto	59.8	22.7	62.5	16.6	43.1	30.2
Molson's	85.5	26.8	43.7	10.4	34.1	16.8
Nationale	25.6	33.1	....	....	66.8	21.3
British Columbia	35.9	27.8	26.7	40.2	190.8	48.2
Dominion	86.2	18.1	71.3	15.5	37.2	40.4
Imperial	79.6	22.4	36.7	11.7	43.5	40.3
Ontario	68.1	22.	35.	10.2	39.3	28.5
Eastern Townships	57.2	38.1	29.	11.6	52.	15.2
Du Peuple	66.8	24.9	25.	7.2	36.2	24.6
Union of Canada	72.3	45.4	4.2	1.4	35.7	7.3
Nova Scotia	94.6	25.6	35.9	12.1	45.9	39.9
Standard	62.5	18.7	34.	9.9	39.2	33.
Hamilton	88.9	37.2	34.	10.1	39.7	18.
Ottawa	77.	39.1	31.	11.6	48.8	22 8
Merchants' of Halifax	93.2	37.8	16.	5.8	42.1	42.
Hochelaga	76.2	54.8	14.1	5.6	45.1	23.
People's of Halifax	22.1	27.3	7.5	5.	71.8	50.5
Traders'	90.7	53.8	2.	.7	33.8	15.1
New Brunswick	84.9	32.7	70.	22.7	55.1	56.4
Jacques Cartier	81.8	35.3	28.	12.	54.8	22.9
Halifax Banking Co	92.3	34.1	20.	5.1	30.5	10.3
Union of Halifax	28.7	26.5	8.	5.7	76.6	67.1
Ville Marie	86.	53.7	4.2	1.9	48.	12 9
Western	87.1	42.	10.6	3.7	38.3	9.8
Yarmouth	20.5	18.5	10.	5.8	64.	27.4
Commercial of Manitoba	99.1	64.8	7.2	3.	44.3	26.8
St. Hyacinthe	68.7	35.6	....	....	37.2	9.3
Comm'l of Windsor, N.S.	21.1	27.2	25.	18.5	92.7	12 9
Exchange of Yarmouth	14.1	62.7	12.2	11.9	109.5	72.7
St. Jean	27.1	134.2	4.4	3.9	91.2	22.
St. Stephen's	83.6	119.6	12.5	5.5	49.9	10.6

ANALYSIS OF BANK STATEMENTS, 31st MARCH, 1888.

BANKS. (In order of amount of paid-up Capital.)	PERCENTAGE OF					
	Cir-culation to Capital.	Circulation to Deposits.	Rest to Capital.	Rest to Disc'nts.	Capital and Rest to Disc'nts.	Cash and Convertible Securities to Circulation and Deposits.
Montreal	46.2	27.8	50.	35.4	106.1	59.5
Commerce	40.8	23.3	8.3	3.6	46.6	31.
Merchants'	53.8	38.7	29.3	13.5	59.7	32.1
British N. America	23.3	18.3	24.1	14.8	76.2	44.5
Quebec	28.7	15.7	13.	5.9	51.2	25.4
Toronto	58.2	21.8	62.5	15.6	40.5	25.6
Molson's	82.5	25.3	43.7	10.2	33.4	16.6
Nationale	25.2	27.9	....	....	65.	22.8
British Columbia	26.9	27.9	20.	38.9	233.7	44.9
Dominion	86.6	18.2	71.3	15.7	37.7	41.
Imperial	79.9	22.7	36.7	11.3	42.1	38.8
Ontario	72.2	23.5	35.	9.9	38.	27.5
Eastern Townships	57.7	39.6	28.9	11.5	51.1	14.2
Du Peuple	79.8	30.4	25.	7.1	35.3	24.
Union of Canada	72.5	40.	4.2	1.4	35.6	17.
Nova Scotia	97.1	27.5	35.9	11.2	42.4	35.9
Standard	61.7	18.8	34.	9.6	38.	30.2
Hamilton	87.9	37.3	34.	9.9	39.	14.6
Ottawa	83.6	42.6	31.	10.8	45.5	22.3
Merchants' of Halifax	95.6	38.8	16.	5.6	40.7	39.5
Hochelaga	85.9	56.9	14.1	5.3	42.8	23.2
People's of Halifax	22.3	30.6	7.5	4.9	70.8	40.6
Traders'	87.6	49.9	2.	.7	35.	22.1
New Brunswick	95.	40.7	70.	21.7	52.8	50.4
Jacques Cartier	95.1	40.9	28.	11.5	52.7	20.1
Halifax Banking Co	88.	32.7	20.	5.2	31.1	11.7
Union of Halifax	30.4	28.3	8.	5.2	70.7	51.5
Ville Marie	91.	56.8	4.2	1.9	47.3	11.9
Western	83.2	40.9	15.2	5.2	39.3	19.3
Yarmouth	24.1	19.2	10.	5.8	64.	32.8
Commercial of Manitoba	93.4	57.1	7.2	3.	44.5	24.7
St. Hyacinthe	74.	36.6	....	....	35.1	10.
Comm'l of Windsor, N.S	22.9	29.8	25.	17.7	88.4	12.8
Exchange of Yarmouth	14.2	60.5	12.2	11.4	104.7	67.1
St. Jean	24.9	121.6	4.4	3.6	86.2	17.7
St Stephen's	84.2	144.9	12.5	5.6	51.	8.5

www.ingramcontent.com/pod-product-compliance
Lightning Source LLC
Chambersburg PA
CBHW022030190326
41519CB00010B/1650